One Year of Desire

poems by

Sarah D'Stair

Finishing Line Press
Georgetown, Kentucky

One Year of Desire

Copyright © 2021 by Sarah D'Stair
ISBN 978-1-64662-718-9 First Edition
All rights reserved under International and Pan-American Copyright Conventions. No part of this book may be reproduced in any manner whatsoever without written permission from the publisher, except in the case of brief quotations embodied in critical articles and reviews.

ACKNOWLEDGMENTS

"Callous," "Between Contradiction," and "Belly" in *Waxing and Waning*, Issue 7, 2021
"A Glance in the Afternoon" in *Jonah Magazine*, 2018
"We Labor in Straight Lines" in *The Ibis Head Review*, 2017
"Walking with Children" and "Landscape with Mutilation" in *The Charles Carter*, 2017
"There is Little Known of Peace" in *Damselfly Press*, 2016
"Evolution" in *Burningword*, 2016

Publisher: Leah Huete de Maines
Editor: Christen Kincaid
Cover Art: ID 146780278 © Janos Gaspar | Dreamstime.com
Author Photo: @2021 Molly Schlachter
Cover Design: Elizabeth Maines McCleavy

Order online: www.finishinglinepress.com
also available on amazon.com

Author inquiries and mail orders:
Finishing Line Press
PO Box 1626
Georgetown, Kentucky 40324
USA

Table of Contents

Evolution 1
Callous 2
Memoir of a Street Serenade 3
Brief, Light 4
There Is Little Known of Peace 5
Meditation 6
Belly 7
Perception of Scent 8
We Labor in Straight Lines 9
Between Contradiction 10
Belly II 11
Midnight 12
Landscape #324 13
A Glance in the Afternoon 14
Articulation 15
Cemetery Walk 16
The Offering 17
Middle Age 18
Landscape with Mutilation 19
Birds Who Fly Low to the Ground 21
Bookstore 22
Waiting Room 23
Rest 24
Seen/Unseen 25
The Art of Foot and Soil 26
Walking with Children 27
Potential Energy 29
Getting to Know Oneself, Again 30

Evolution

It's in the way Glenn Gould's lips move
around the notes
sound reaching out into air, just
beyond him
he must catch it
draw it back into his body
tight and bent

in the attack of even the most piano
of pianos which bores down center
lost and falling and weighted
then flits out, released from the
dark, the moment just before the sound

that moment, there
before sound happens,
trapped within flakes of snow
on a cold still day, disturbed

the unending battle
between hands, which one gets the
moment before sound,
and which after,
which demands the sharp
which the fifth
which the fattest chord
which the sostenuto

we are vocal chords and
we are plucked chords
we are the vibrato of body at seeming rest
here we become most primal
closest to the earth and of necessity
without sight

Callous

A tuft of odd skin
wrung hand pulled tight
a consciousness of body
from the very beginning
emerges like a nest
built quick then washed away.
An extravagance of skin
regret an aching, aging vibration
fingertips balance the bald universe
hold unfelled trees up straight
tend to children and dying flowers.
We pull and beg and grip and swear
we mourn ourselves ugly
mourn ourselves lost, mourn
shamefaced an emboldened caress
we enchant and scoff
hold fast a ridicule, we find apex
in a parody of the unseen.

Memoir of a Street Serenade

Mid-winter chill, the lingering
haunt of word, chord, glass.

Old desire grounds us into long
evenings, useless, fastidious wanting
dusty avenues, opines, heavy eyes
that drag into tomorrow.

We are the scraps a stray ant left behind
on its way to a meaningful life,
we watch it forge its straight line
on the tips of grassy blades.

This sense of ourselves, this want,
inward, social, an untraced heartbeat,
a secret moment, when the trees feel
themselves your best friends,
or the hum of Glenn Gould's Bach
finds its way into your throat,
like those lunch hours spent
reading "The Lady of Shalott" aloud
on a San Francisco street corner,
sheer exuberance voiced stentorian
in the streets, onlookers pass without
glance, which emboldens the rhymes
out into the city air.

Brief, Light

Swollen grey sky, dusted treetops,
the white field a monolith,
frozen, windless morning.
The ground underneath, frozen, too,
exposed where the little dog, excited
and jumping, traced himself beneath the trees.
The sun hesitates today.
Only a single lamplight, wide, distorted,
sleepy, fails the unlit expanse.
Noticed, the light goes out.
Wildness returns, great aching beauty
barely seen, visible for a moment from a
far off place, imprecise, suspended,
it returns to its heavy mysteries.

There Is Little Known of Peace

we look for it in
sodden sole-weathered feet

in hot shrill cicada mornings
and field-empty crow evenings

in the weather-worn salt of day
the punch prose weakness of night

tumbling hands as they
sway astride the body

grave frostbitten eyes
that remain shut

while the news of the world
carries on unknown

while the days of the world carry on

in pop-gun attitudes
the croak of an old cat's meow

slam-shut screen doors at the
hands of hurried children

there are too few clean lines

we need each word of the day
slow and full in the mouth

Meditation

the mind folds in on itself
tucked in like creased felt
pursued corner to corner
inverted tight into the recessed
least lit corner of the room

one small unlit edge
surrounded by lesser darkness
both finite and infinite
all directions dim
and shudder

matter gives way to moment
inclination to silence

the cicada's electric roar
now the throat that issues
our own voice
the cat's hoarse moan
the light transcribed
on our own eyes
the thunderous overhead
a release of tight breath from
our own lungs

Belly

My belly is a small town
in which I dwell
in earthly celebration.
The sign and symbol
of all my delights.
My belly expands in
depth and precision
like lines of poetry
crafted from morning
coffee, without boundary
or superstition or delay.
The end of my days will
be filled with it, admiring,
amused in its verse.
Ode to belly, my west
wind, my intellectual beauty,
my mean flower and ruined
abbey, my Mont Blanc.
Like Ben Bulben it towers
over Yeats' endless witticism.
Watch it issue forth, this
belly, this happy occasion,
let loose on the world
let loose your imagination,
see my child smile, see the
growth of his soul, the hand
of my lover in caress.
My belly follows me into the
bath. I magnify its eloquence.
Its space and strength respond
heartily to my Yes.

Perception of Scent

A gluttony of roses drink
the body's glory into its breath.
Nearby, a kitten's tail bristles
out pure chemical desire.

Fingertips dip into creek beds, inert,
while streamwater lunges toward the future
wrapped around a tadpole's body.
Even the concrete steps feel us stumble,
wonder if we are desperate or merely clumsy,
ground and grounded, reciprocal.

We half touch the earth,
half the rhythm is ours, half the texture.
The equation runs its course.
It consoles us from our knowing,
outlines us in silhouette,
our shape, its curve.

The very air is alive,
enfolds us womb-like as we roam
the open field
or sit in our kitchens,
a closed envelope with us inside
while we see with our bipedal eyes
into the distance.

We Labor in Straight Lines

We labor in straight lines—
book pages, church spires, cigarettes,
bridges that span unpredictable seas.

They are the gods of symmetry,
the bending of curved nature
to our straight-edged whims.

They are our holy sonnets,
proclamations of complex desire,
the worship of abandoned hope.
Abandon all hope, they say.

They are the fonted alphabets relieved
of some shaky hand, and they are
framed yellow wings.

(We favor vibrato for respite.)

They are the stilts that hold our tiny souls
above the rushing tide.

Between Contradiction

Between the black bishop and the white
is an ecstasy of disobedience.
A question mark sits round and plump like
my belly, at the edge of precipice, obstinate,
like words written by Gertrude Stein.

Belly II

Belly, I celebrate you
wide you hang over my underclothes
deep as a thundercloud
firm like a feral cat tracing its
unassuming prey
you set the intention for the day
you guide the arms that breathless
attempt to subdue you
firm and thick and solid
you spite gravity
you hold the earth at bay
you control the tides that wash me away
far out into the sea
you dart your eyes and see me
reach my hand out from the dashing waves
and you wave back with a sly smile
you sit back in your armchair and wait
for me to make it back ashore
you wait with patient abandon
simmering in your own persistence
you kindle the fire that sets my path ablaze
I turn my eyes to you always
always swim back to you breathless
naked wild bewildered.

Midnight

The mind drifts into its own sway
in the dark night, like the bench
where I sat with my first true love.
We talked about TV shows and held
hands, fingertip to fingertip in the
moonlight, yellowed light, a fog.
The earth held us in its cradled arms
such a sweet long time ago.

A walk at midnight, a slight hill,
you smile back at me a little,
breathless but hiding it.
Or the first time we lay side by side,
air pulsating with the life we will share.

Sacred yellow fog, the heavy air
lingers, pulls us closer, present, alive
in the winter night. We tell scary stories
near the railroad tracks,
we make each other laugh.

Still the air is thick, the moon slight,
we cross under a bridge,
there are ghosts in the trees,
myths they will tell someday.

Like the song I sang when you asked,
a christmas song, I didn't know any others.
You said I had a beautiful voice.
It was a truth born of days that hold their own
magic, their own suffering,
wild panicked love.

But this night, full of desire,
suspended in memory like the fog
itself, encircles us, gives us a reason
to keep searching, hands outstretched.

Landscape #324

This morning, a lovely pastel
pink tree line frames the field.
The sun is rising.
The field, slivered into pieces,
long bands of melted snow
reveals rust colored earth.
Smokestacks steam excess,
trees turn opaque,
unconcerned, they stand tall
and reaching.

The colors of day, memories,
young and brazen, slipping into
places we should not be,
denuded first kiss, half
remembered, almost lost,
cool sheets at nighttime,
unnamed faces, books,
alphabets, pale slender hands
at rest atop yellowed piano keys.

A Glance in the Afternoon

a dozen limp roses crackle with dust
on the bedside table, rotten with
fallen leaves and dewy residue

caroline should be the name
of a flower children suck the sweetness from

I remember my own sweet little friend

an imagined embrace in the flesh of my arms
pushed against the wall of sweet honeysuckle

later that day
picnic table conversations pierced our wild faces

Articulation

in our hands soggy paper
drawings of limp faces, ragged outlines
(our own faces, too, ragged)

the words sing all over
they shout
and they shout

the paper is damp with neglect
granite outlines silhouetted
old faces turned down

here, we lay on the floor
our backs crooked
legs firm to the ground
flesh spread out in celebration

and look for words littered
all over scraps of paper
claw toward pale letters

then look for the alphabet,
another world we can climb

write these lines too deeply
the words are lost behind each other

we press pale lives between letters
that crawl over our prostate bodies
escape just as we find them
steal away fast before fingertips can grip them
scramble off to small houses
leave our frail bodies sullen
collapsed exhausted

Cemetery Walk

Across a two-lane highway, near to my house,
a walking path begins among headstones,
mossy facades, memories of laughter, or grimace.
I step vaguely afraid, with circulating blood,
along the path to older stones, aging along with me,
infant twins among them from the last century.

The path turns, lavishes the remnants of an ancient
stone cottage, now a museum, meticulously restored
for public viewing, an honest work-for-show farm.
Here, the dead and living, untethered from necessity,
step together under a vast canopy of gnarled trees,
all of us crooked under osteopathic bones as the
chipmunks squirrel along just ahead.

Further down the path, marigolds impress a bright
green landscape with prim and proper melodies,
just next to obscure pond water that, on sunny days,
mirrors a dilapidated wooden shed, a horse trough,
duck bills and the noses of two sheep, best old friends,
while flickering tree leaves survey the scene.

On hot summer days, I touch the horses as they seek
refuge in the grove of trees closest to the path,
this close to them I see flies bite at their eyes.
I try to envision a peace thick with waking life.

The Offering

Listen to those solitary notes,
one slow step at a time,
footsteps going up, going down,
climbing, each one climbing,
not in a clamor, but a nod.

Look past the gluttonous chords,
see instead the lonely ones, plucked
melodic, B natural, C, down to G,
perfect time, perfect space,
no question, no pause to question.

Here is where the mind is composed.
You will find plumbed depths there
under each key, right there, underneath.

We must press down solid, square,
each note depressed, full, heavy.
It is no time for chords.
No time for discord either.

We must resonate out soft and deep and alone,
clear beneath the layered voices over top.

Middle Age

I grow old, Prufrock says.
It's in the way I laugh.

All the life I once held inward,
silent, crystalline in heartache,
now makes known its simple,
insuperable desires.

All of it, suspicious,
silent knowing, unmoving,
except a slight breeze,
a small respite.

We want to rest firm
rooted and swaying,
slightly unaware of why.
We want to find blue flowers,
dance across a long bridge,
begin again from today.

Landscape with Mutilation

One sees death
for the first time
as bees glaze
across the windowpane,
glass framing
the picture like Giotto
framed the
descent into hell,
bodies contorted
in perfectly parabolic
brushstrokes while
demon beasts lick
genitals
with their tails.

Here
the dizzied vermin body
begs from one branch
to the next, his canvas
oversaturated,
yellowed
from too much green,
branches mangled parabola
like Giotto's bodies as they
swell into each other

while below, an upstart wren
nicks her beak responsibly
into the soil
even as her birdmates
lift away, off to seek
another pleasure.

And that large blot
of brownblack
behind the slight
flecked leaves?
One can make out
a red-tailed hawk,
the solitary shifting eye.

The chase lasts only a moment.
The bright denizens
of that lonely place watch
the small body clawed,
flayed alive, flesh tendrilled.

End scene. And I wonder,
is there a martyr in this
painted mystery play?

Birds Who Fly Low to the Ground

On a quiet summer morning,
the greenblack of one tree
frames the yellowed leaves of another.

Quick, slight birds whip round
in low circles, nearly touch the earth,
singular yet synonymous,
alone and coupled, they fly off
in perfectly tailored synchrony.

They indulge in paradox.
Each circle round, a collision,
a collusion, a work ethic,
an idle moment, a haughty boast,
two deferential nods.

Bookstore

Fingertips to tongue
give the page a full wet embrace.

This place is full of wonders.

Aisles of lovers,
philosophy, fairy tales,
the meeting of two minds,
full of silence,
full of words,
wistful abandon,
deadened sorrow.
And how shall the two meet?

Footsteps escape, rest, quiver along
head slightly nodded to the right,
spines themselves elude the seeing.

Like in a vineyard
plucking grapes
sneaking one or two along the way.

Waiting Room

We first hear the words
in the dull glowing light
eyes hollow and looking
for places to rest

the ones looking are the
only bodies in the room
we hear the doctor's hollow
boots of polished patent leather

we sit still cold alone
bones aching along the collar
we leave ourselves behind
others hobble behind us
we smile naked
the air seeps from our lonely skin

we mistake other shadows for our own
wish for the weight of fine clothes
silky shaded lace stockings

hallway half smiles
tiny letters on white paper
are all the same after all

women at long tables with
glasses on their noses carry plans
they pass along to us
thick with irony, subtle humor

wide angle photographs
memories we force on ourselves
smiles and a stranger's neck
fingers tentative in their light grasp

Rest

A rest is a rhythmic event.
One leg outside the
blanket, one leg in.

Rest belly, rest eyes,
subdue your forethought,
require the future
but leave the present
alone, stay on the mountain,
though you're supposed
to come down, think
what permission is given to
every child's dream,
the monkey bars hold us still,
the merry-go-round, slides.

Animals watch and wave
in three-quarter time.
This event, also a rest.

Seen/Unseen

A cat sleeps with a frozen appetite
or claws the window, squirrels chased
through glass, a filmic quarantine.

A determined hawk flays a passing bunny.
The heron at the creek finds sediment
wriggling with delicious life.
The fox dashes into the open field,
then disappears, quick as our questions.

Muffled birdsong, sweet and away,
reminds us of the flowers we so carefully
forgot to plant.

The Art of Foot and Soil

First you must escape
slip out from the darkened room
then trail out beyond engine hum echoes

find the small worn footpath
over the vast dead field

arrive at dusk's light
listen carefully

you will hear the swell
of vast veined oceans
the pulse of plucked feathers
aching mountaintops
skeleton flesh limestone
the gluttoned earth singing
of tongue and soil

hear the soft water
melodic in its lullaby
the next breath you are afraid to take

Walking with Children

> *"I am trying to get at something utterly heartbroken."*
> —*Vincent Van Gogh to his brother Theo, c/o Annie Dillard*

One must draw out the poetry.
One must sketch it with chalk on the long, lonely blacktop.

First, the path. It is bridled
with bugs. A story ensues. Two bugs
were stuck together. It was an ant
carrying his dead friend
like a crumb of fallen bread.
(I am informed that ants die, too.)
This one was helping his friend
back to life.

Second, the spider. Her web spans
the footbridged brook.
One must direct the gaze into
empty space to find it. Not into the water,
but above it.
An optical abstraction.
The web is found, sun-glimpsed,
suspended.
The mystery: how did she propel
that first strand
across the water?
It is a genesis question.
I cannot answer.

We continue. We see two ducks
standing motionless
along the path.
(He, pleased, corrects me—
not ducks. Geese.)
On approach, our bodies
crouch a little,

gaits tiptoe with respect.
Shh…we say.
The mysteries, we say to each other,
accumulate along this path. Still,
the geese do not move.
A little closer.
I see first, then he, that after all
they are not alive.
And that mystery is solved.
Someone has placed stone
geese in live action poses
along this footpath.
The deeper puzzle: Why?

And now the walk is long.
The path is long.
I am curious where it ends.
He is not.
He finds a stick to pass the time.
We fall into silence.

The pavement ends, and we follow
a narrow dirt trail
deeper into the woods.
I am asked if the birds mind
us being here.

Just after, the path forks into three.
I choose a way for us.
He says, "We're lost, in an outside tunnel."

Potential Energy

potential energy excels
in its own absence

box and whisker plots
perfect median outliers

formulas that find the fall
of gravity

the first sip of coffee in the morning
lungs heavy with heartbreak

the kick to a bicycle stand
first leg off the bed in the morning

sternum open wide for the coming breath

Getting to Know Oneself, Again

melancholy, quiet,
this getting to know oneself, again

reflected light on bath tiles
while reading a long-paged book
where have you been these past
twenty years

a cat's tongue tricks the skin into
crooked places, lounging, splayed
on the living room floor
we lay there as long as we want

spectacles, in an odd place today,
will be there tomorrow
only one's own clothes
in the Sunday afternoon wash

all this quiet, craven, craved,
died for, blighted
only oneself to thank
pale shadows bidden onto walls
across from the old chandelier

eyes rest on a chair no one has sat in
pillows rest only one's own head
words tiny madnesses under weight
of cups and toasts with cheese
served alongside purple plums
revered from a long time ago

these moments, minute and vast
compose the length of one's intellect
sense, strength

the organized body bursts out into
the fast-reveling world
it soaks in insouciant footsteps

eyes find the wind, the green grass
on hills farther than we can see

Sarah D'Stair is the author of *Central Valley* (Kuboa Press, 2017). Her poetry and short fiction have appeared in numerous journals, and she reviews poetry for *The Adroit Journal, The Rupture Magazine* and elsewhere. She received her Ph.D. in English from the University of Massachusetts, Amherst, and publishes academic articles in the field of literature and critical animal studies. She lives and teaches in Lancaster, Pennsylvania.

www.ingramcontent.com/pod-product-compliance
Lightning Source LLC
LaVergne TN
LVHW041507070426
835507LV00012B/1396